Lots of things
you want to know about
KNIGHTS
...and some
you don't!

Written and Illustrated by
David West

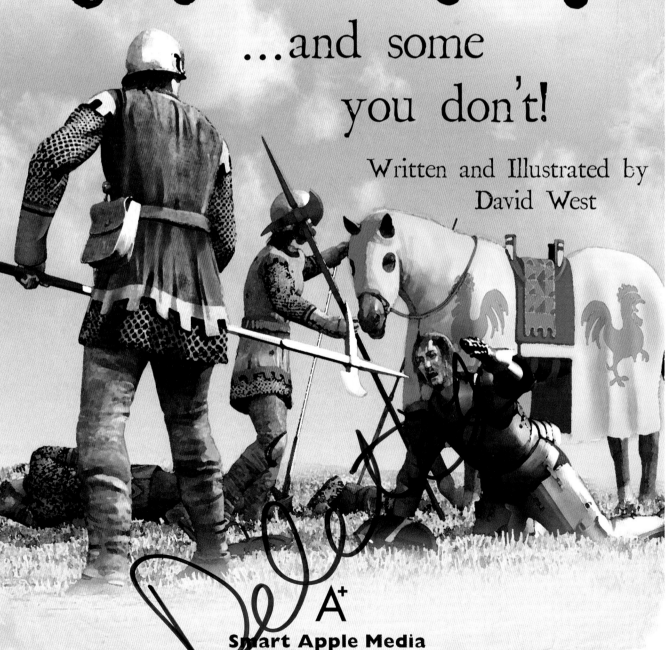

A⁺
Smart Apple Media

Published by Smart Apple Media, an imprint of Black Rabbit Books
P.O. Box 3263, Mankato, Minnesota 56002
www.smartapplemedia.com

Produced by David West ㅈㅈ Children's Books
6 Princeton Court, 55 Felsham Road, London SW15 1AZ

Designed and illustrated by David West

Copyright © 2013 David West Children's Books

Library of Congress Cataloging-in-Publication Data

West, David, 1956-
Lots of things you want to know about knights : ... and some you don't! / David West.
pages cm. – (Lots of things you want to know about)
Includes index.
ISBN 978-1-62588-091-8
1. Knights and knighthood–Europe–History–Juvenile literature. 2. Civilization, Medieval–Juvenile literature.
3. Chivalry–Europe–History–Juvenile literature. I. Title.
CR4513.W46 2015
929.7'4–dc23
2013030730
Printed in China
CPSIA compliance information DWCB15CP
311214

9 8 7 6 5 4 3 2 1

Contents

The First Knights Wore Chainmail Armor

The rank of knight developed from the mounted warriors of the 10th and 11th centuries. These early mounted warriors came from the ruling classes. They were armored with chainmail, carefully constructed garments of interlinking rings of metal.

The Last Knights Wore Plate Armor

By the end of the 14th century, knights wore suits of full plates of armor. Plate armor was virtually invulnerable to sword slashes. They did have weak points at the joints, which long pointed swords and weapons, such as a **pollaxe** or **halberd,** could penetrate.

Knights Fought on Horseback

Horses were extremely important, and each knight owned several. Their war horses were known as chargers. Knights generally fought other knights and viewed foot soldiers as troublesome obstacles on the way to their enemy.

Captured Knights Could Be Ransomed

If a knight was taken prisoner, his life was often spared by his captors. They realized that a knight was worth more alive than dead. Knights were held for **ransom**, usually in comfortable surroundings. This did not apply to other warriors, such as archers and foot soldiers, who were often killed after capture.

Knights Hunted with Birds

Falconry was a popular sport for knights and kings in the **Middle Ages**. A trained bird of prey, such as a goshawk, was launched after animals like rabbits, hares, and game birds.

Knights also enjoyed hunting for wild boar on horseback with spears.

A Lady Was a Knight's Wife

When a knight married, his wife was given the title of Lady. Some women became knights in their own right. In 1149, the count of Barcelona honored the women who defended the town of Tortosa with a military order of knighthood.

Knights Lived in Castles

Knights lived in the castles of the lord or noble they served. Much of their time was spent practicing weapons skills and horsemanship. Knights might also accompany the lord hunting. Part of their time was also spent studying the rules of **chivalry**.

Knights in Training Were Called Squires

Future knights were sent away to a castle to be pages. Young boys served as pages for seven years, running messages and cleaning. At 14 they became a squire. As well as learning to fight, a squire had other duties. One was dressing the knight for combat.

Knights Sometimes Fought Their Friends

During the Middle Ages, knights often met up at tournaments to compete with friends in chivalrous competitions, or mock battles. One of the events was jousting, in which two mounted knights rode at each other and tried to knock their opponent from the saddle with a lance.

William Marshal Was the Greatest Tournament Knight

The younger son of a minor nobleman, William Marshal had to make his own way in life, as he had no fortune to inherit. Valuable prizes and money could be won by ransoming opponents captured in tournaments. At the time of his death, William had beaten 500 knights during his tournament career.

Knights Were Recognized by Their Coats of Arms

Designs containing **heraldic beasts** and other symbols were used by knights as a form of recognition. They were called coats of arms because they were applied to a shield, **surcoat,** and even a horse's **caparison**.

Squires Were Hit with a Sword When Knighted

A squire could be knighted by another knight, a noble, or even the king. The king would hit the squire on the back with the flat of his sword. This was called dubbing and was accompanied by the words, "I dub thee sir (name of knight)."

Knights Had a Code of Conduct Called Chivalry

As well as training to fight, knights had to follow a chivalric code. They were required to be gentle and gracious to all women, to have virtues such as mercy, courage, valor, and fairness, to protect the weak and poor, and to serve their lord.

Knights Went on Crusades

Western knights were bound by their chivalric code to defend the church. Kings and lords from Western Europe encouraged their knights to join them on quests to regain Jerusalem from Muslim armies. These crusades continued throughout the 11th, 12th, and 13th centuries.

Some Knights Belonged to Religious Orders

Templar knights, in their distinctive white robes with a red cross, were among the most skilled warriors of the crusades. They were a **monastic** order, raised to defend pilgrims visiting the Holy Land from bandits.

Faris Were Arabian Knights

Horse-riding warriors in the Middle East called "Faris" studied "furusiyya," which can be compared to European chivalry. Their military exercises included horsemanship, archery, and charging with a lance.

Faris were also trained in wrestling, chess, and the arts of war and hunting.

Samurai Were Japanese Knights

Samurai were the military nobles of Japan. They followed a set of rules called "bushido," which means "the way of the warrior." The code stressed frugality, loyalty, martial arts mastery, and honor. If a samurai failed to uphold his honor, he could regain it by performing seppuku (ritual suicide).

Joan of Arc Led the French Army to Victory

Born a peasant girl in 1412, Joan claimed divine guidance. Although she was not a knight, she wore armor and led the French army to many victories against the English. She was eventually captured and found guilty of **heresy** and burned at the stake at the age of 19.

Glossary

caparison a cloth covering a horse

chivalry a code of conduct involving honor, gallantry, and individual training and service

halberd an ax blade topped with a spike mounted on a long shaft

heraldic beasts stylized animals, birds, and mythical creatures used on coats of arms

heresy a belief or idea contrary to the religion of the time

Middle Ages a period of European history that lasted from the 5th until the 15th centuries

monastic relating to, or of, a monastery

pollaxe similar to a halberd but with a smaller ax head

ransom demanding money for a prisoner's release

surcoat an outer garment worn over the armor of a knight

Index

A
armor 4, 5, 22

C
caparison 15

castle 10

chainmail 4

charger 6

chivalry 10, 12, 17, 18, 20

coat of arms 15

crusade 18, 19

F
falconry 8

faris 20

H
halberd 5

heraldry 15

heresy 22

hunting 8, 10, 20

J
Joan of Arc 22

jousting 12

L
Lady 9

lance 12, 20

M
Marshal, William 14

Middle Ages 8, 12

monastic 19

P
pollaxe 5

R
ransom 7, 14

S
samurai 21

squire 11, 16

surcoat 15

T
Templar 19

tournament 12, 14

W
wild boar 8